Cemetery Jamboree

Deborah Kadair Thomas

PELICAN PUBLISHING COMPANY

GRETNA 2016

The word "Pelican" and the depiction of a pelican are
trademarks of Pelican Publishing Company, Inc., and are
registered in the U.S. Patent and Trademark Office.

ISBN: 9781455622399
E-book ISBN: 9781455622405

Printed in Malaysia
Published by Pelican Publishing Company, Inc.
1000 Burmaster Street, Gretna, Louisiana 70053

To Bob—thank you for always believing in me

To Sally Boitnott—thank you for the gentle nudge

In New Orleans on Halloween night,
the dearly departed sway in
the moonlight.
They gather their bones and they set
'em just right.
The cemetery jamboree starts tonight!

A call comes out for the spirits to come;
they start arriving one by one.
Who will appear? No one knows.
As the moon gets high,
the crowd grows and grows.

Louis Armstrong is the first to show.
Trumpet in hand, he gives it a blow.
It reminds his soul of bygone days.
Once he gets started, he plays
and plays.

In New Orleans on Halloween night,
the dearly departed sway in
the moonlight.
They gather their bones and they set
'em just right.
The cemetery jamboree starts tonight!

Mahalia Jackson hears the call.
She arrives on cue for this ghostly ball.
She clears her throat and starts to sing.
You can tell she's an angel—just
look at those wings.

In New Orleans on Halloween night,
the dearly departed sway in
the moonlight.
They gather their bones and they set
'em just right.
The cemetery jamboree starts tonight!

Drifting up next is Marie Laveau.
You can be sure she wouldn't
miss this show.
If she gets the chance, she'll cast a spell.
Magic's her art and she does it well.

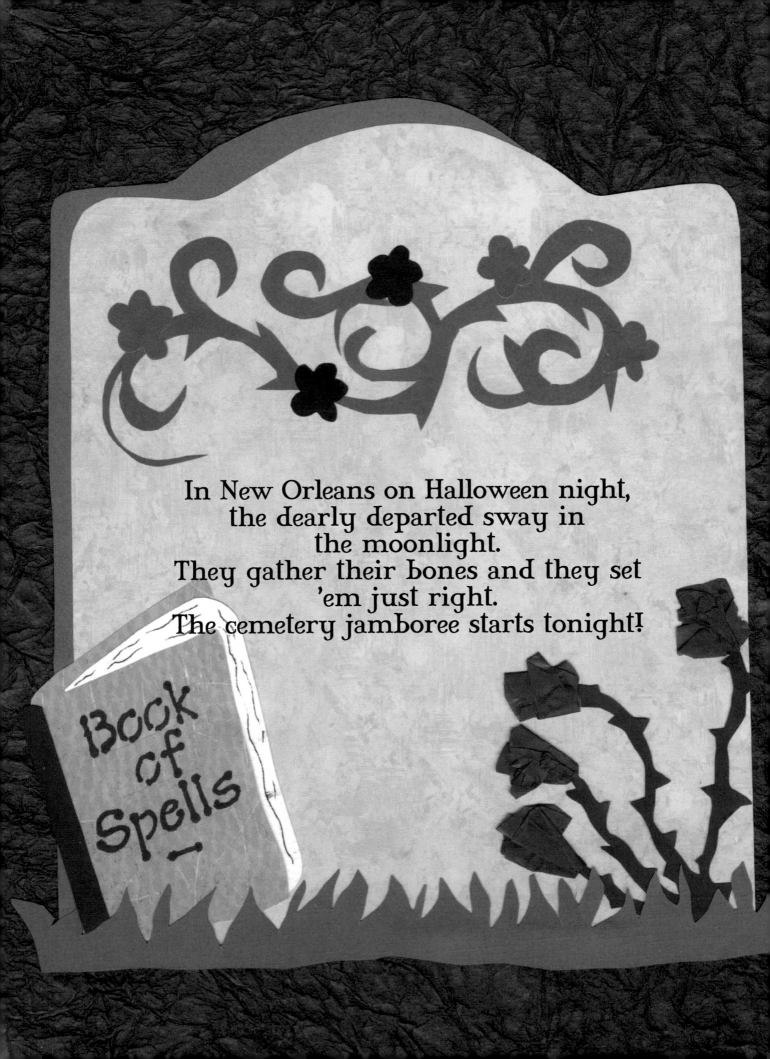

In New Orleans on Halloween night,
the dearly departed sway in
the moonlight.
They gather their bones and they set
'em just right.
The cemetery jamboree starts tonight!

Book of Spells

Andrew Jackson rides up on
his steed.
It's a spectacular sight, all
have agreed.
He rallies his troops for a search
to begin—
"Look high and low for the souls
of lost men."

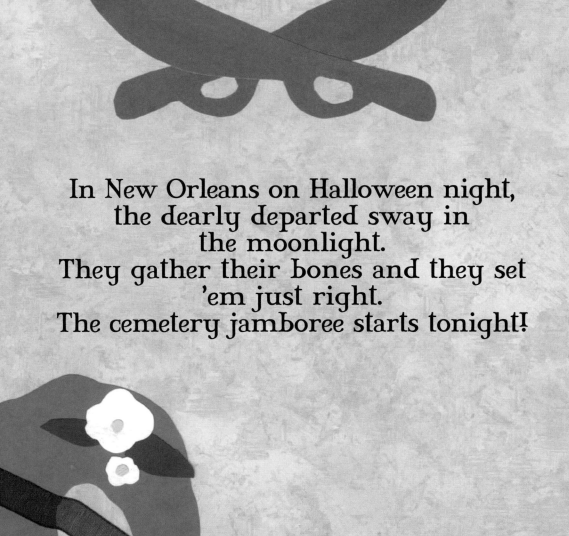

In New Orleans on Halloween night,
the dearly departed sway in
the moonlight.
They gather their bones and they set
'em just right.
The cemetery jamboree starts tonight!

Jean Lafitte yells, "Land ho!"
He arrives with his crew in tow.
He surveys the scene—the
spirits abound.
Never before was such
treasure found.

In New Orleans on Halloween night,
the dearly departed sway in
the moonlight.
They gather their bones and they set
'em just right.
The cemetery jamboree starts tonight!

Huey P. Long arrives in style,
gathers a crowd, and stumps
for a while.
He fills those spirits with
promises grand:
"Every man a king," he tells this
loyal band.

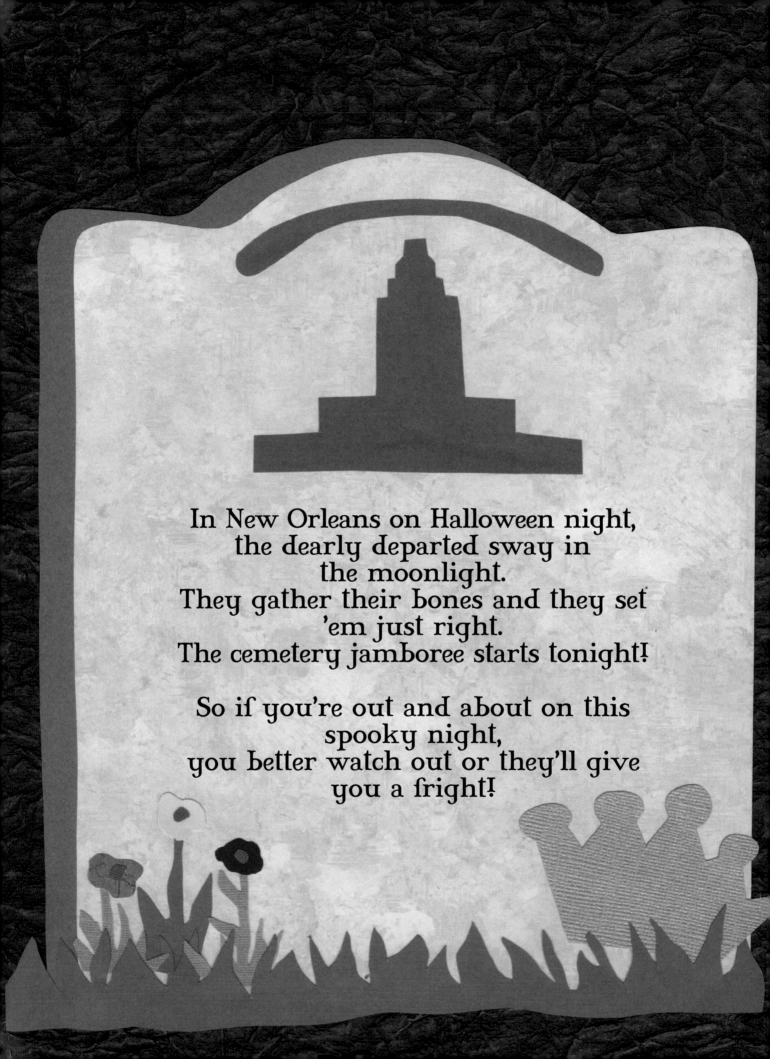

In New Orleans on Halloween night,
the dearly departed sway in
the moonlight.
They gather their bones and they set
'em just right.
The cemetery jamboree starts tonight!

So if you're out and about on this
spooky night,
you better watch out or they'll give
you a fright!

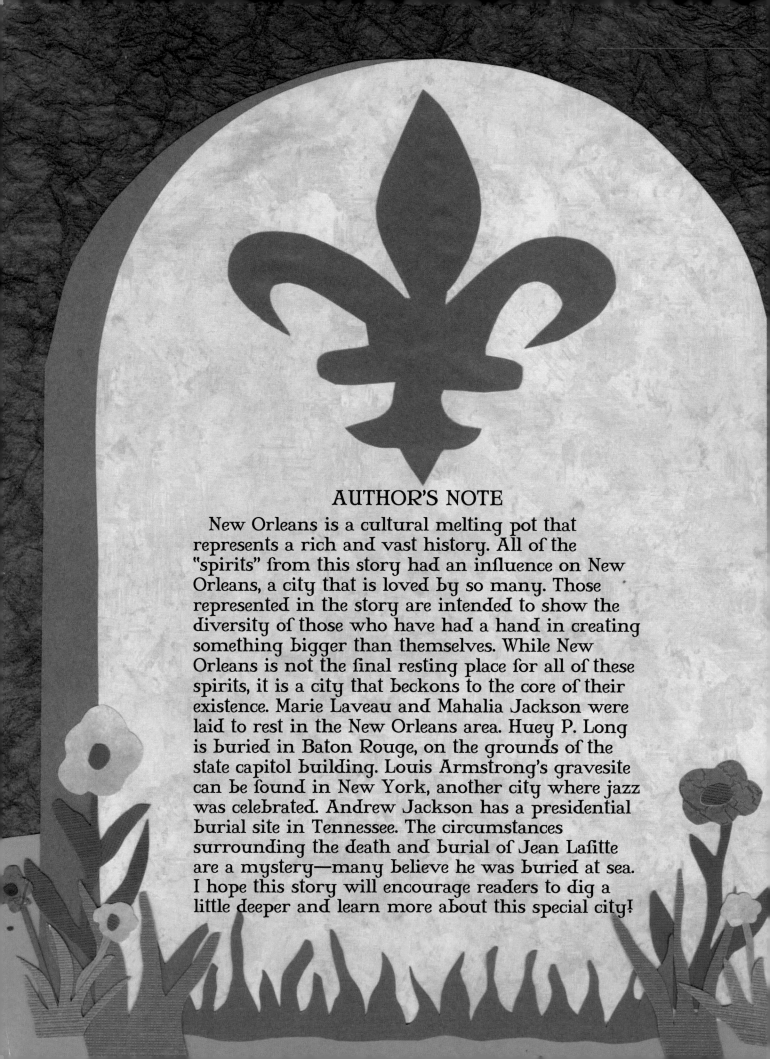

AUTHOR'S NOTE

New Orleans is a cultural melting pot that represents a rich and vast history. All of the "spirits" from this story had an influence on New Orleans, a city that is loved by so many. Those represented in the story are intended to show the diversity of those who have had a hand in creating something bigger than themselves. While New Orleans is not the final resting place for all of these spirits, it is a city that beckons to the core of their existence. Marie Laveau and Mahalia Jackson were laid to rest in the New Orleans area. Huey P. Long is buried in Baton Rouge, on the grounds of the state capitol building. Louis Armstrong's gravesite can be found in New York, another city where jazz was celebrated. Andrew Jackson has a presidential burial site in Tennessee. The circumstances surrounding the death and burial of Jean Lafitte are a mystery—many believe he was buried at sea. I hope this story will encourage readers to dig a little deeper and learn more about this special city!